This is dedicated to the ones I love

ISBN: 978-1-906018-09-2

A CIP catalogue for this book is available from the National Library.

Interior photography courtesy of Maureen McDonnell. Interior paintings courtesy of Ann Moloney.

Published by Original Writing Ltd., Ireland, 2007.

CONTENTS

III
PERILS AND GEMS

IV
I WISH

V
WORD PLAY

VI
SIMPLY THE BEST

VII
CUT TO CHASE

ACKNOWLEDGEMENTS

I wish to acknowledge the friends who continually urged me to *do something* with these poems. A special thanks to Ann Moloney, artist, and Maureen McDonnell, photographer for their generosity. I also wish to acknowledge the excellence of IT instructor Anne Moylan, Noreside Education Centre and the kindness of Sinéad Kennedy who first typed the poems in her spare time. Finally thanks to Andrew and Martin Delany of Original Writing Ltd. for the last word in publishing.

I
THAT'S LIFE

That's Life

Tonight I feel I lost a friend
A friend unique
To whom I whispered secrets
In the dark
You do not leave me there
But make it starkly clear
That we are friends no more

No time to talk this out
Or question what it's all about
Do you have to shout it out again?
Why won't I just accept the pain
Realise that feelings change
Nothing of the past remains
Except our four children

On Patrick's Night we had a dance
An evening filled with warm romance and fun
The kind that ends too soon
Within a week and all by chance
You re-interpreted romance
And said that if we'd danced
You danced a different tune.

In bed at night I sense that lost security
What else have I to lose?
Darts of fear distracting me
In that same dark where I distracted you with love
While your heart beat out notes of treachery
And as I ponder which of us is more alone
I switch on to *That's Life* but I don't understand

Alive And Kicking

A Derry man, I can identify
He asks us to recall a day
One you'll remember 'til you die
And please—Mean what you say!

I'll never forget the day
You told me so coldly,
"I don't love you any more."

That sinking feeling
Down, down, down…
No kiss of life, no kiss of death
Just gone!

This world is full of clowns
And I am one alone
I'm on my own

How is it that I don't feel ill?
My zest for life is far from still
I am alive and kicking

Just think he could have picked *me* out
And asked me to recite
That unforgettable day.

Would he have snarled and hurled abuse?
Would I have offered lame excuse
Or let my anger out?

I'll never forget the day
I hugged my mother
As though there were no tomorrow
…She chickens out

I begin again…
I'll never forget the day
He chanced to say
"I don't love you any more"
"When?"
"Yesterday."

II
TRAIN OF THOUGHT

Blotto

"Out, out, damned spot!" she scorned
I think of postbox red for blood
India blue for ink
On pure white blotting paper
So white, so blue
So soft, so indelible
I drank a mouthful of petrol blue once
Straight from the bottle
I must have been thirsting for some peer attention
And it worked
School days are not the same
You can't go all gothic on a highlighter
Even as you disclaim Macbeth.

Adolescent Ecstasy

As lights went out I took delight
In nursing young affections
No wheel of fear can quite compare
With juvenile attraction

I might have been a princess
In a castle where the sea
Saliva lapped the jagged rocks
In style curvaceously

That slowly surging crest of surf
In vertical direction
Crashes once ecstatically
Unleashing sweet sensations

And sweetly I would think of him
As preciously as in a dream
Deciphering each word and glance
To magnify our mute romance

I wonder was I on my own
Within those convent walls
Indulging faithful fantasies
Fulfilling silent voids

I reckon that the nuns had ways
To sooth unspoken pain
Did they romanticise on days
When they were home again?

But back to thoughts more fanciful
And ones that bring a smile
Long before those girlish dreams
Of walking up the aisle

Another Brian fantasy fed my imagination
As we at higher levels now pursued our education
I feel again the adolescent pains and fascinations
The blush and flush, relentless crush, of mental stimulation.

Can you remember what you thought
As you sat next to me
Imparting that the Mournes embraced
Your home place close to sea?

I knew that in a week we'd move
If what you said was true
Was I to spend my whole life long
Contemplating you?

And now sometimes I find that I seek splendid isolation
So I can lose myself in lines bereft of explanation
And blissfully my fantasies emerge with verve and passion
A rhapsody in verse revealing timeless revelation

Skin Deep

Slimming drives me round the twist
All I crave I must resist
I lose a pound, I gain a few
God direct me what to do.

Guilt is such a heavy chore
Especially when I eat some more
Of all those fanciful delights
Go on, let's have another bite

Slimming is the thing to do
Mirrors in the bathroom too
Let me have a proper view
So I shall know what I must do

Who is it that I'm trying to ape?
Why this discomfort with my shape?
Could it be that my self-image doesn't measure up enough?
Should I be made of stronger stuff?

Mirror, Mirror on the wall
Why let you be my downfall?
My destiny is all my own
Don't you remark on how I've grown!

I shall work on what's inside
That's where I have things to hide
Not on what the eye can see
But on the real essential me.

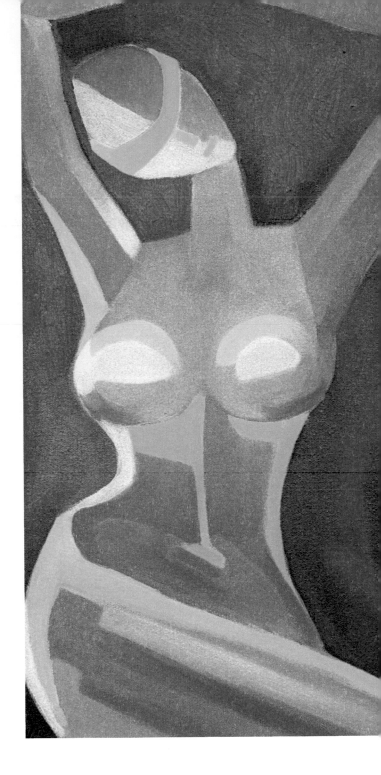

On Broken Dreams

Mirella, fortune-teller extraordinaire
Tells me her tale
Outside, a charming woman in the trade
Inside, a sad woman with a tale
Of personal assault and broken dreams
For Joe was the best when he was sober
Once professional in working out
Who dunnit
Since sobbing in his total disbelief
That it was he
Who brandished a knife
Just inches from their precious son
And discoloured the body of a good woman.

Sad Mirella, but with a spark
That lit up the heart of another man
Who begged to woo her and
Surround her with affection
Why stay with Joe
Destroyer of dreams?
Because it's what she knew
For she was sick like him
And mistakenly believed for him
She was responsible.

Precious Time

When my parents died
I needed time
Time to think
Time to savour
Time to mourn
Their loss in silence.

Day to day
I say a lot
Sometimes mindless tommy rot
Suppressing mutely
Words of mouth
Worth sharing

Time is precious
Family ties
Us up in knots
Not sharing thoughts
Of who or what we are
Or want to be

Mind precious mine
Knowing…needing…
To shop around in search of daily bread
Fresh, not stalemate
Far away from TV dinner, TV dead
Centering on precious thought and word
In time I know we souls will find our soulmates.

Ideals

It only happens now and then
I catch a glimpse of how and when
My hero or my heroine
Is not afraid to stand alone

Bob Geldof, you can take a bow
For moving mountains
God knows how
Or why you are no standerby
Who can allow starvation?

And Dervla, a woman warm
From circling miles in search of charm
Causing sometimes some alarm
Is this a woman or a man
Whose simple courage
Can disarm the natives?

As a baby I am born
So too the moment yet unknown
Nothing written on my face
I'm unique in time and place
Momentarily at least

Will I stretch to touch the dawn?
Or give one huge enormous yawn?
Will my eyelids flutter gaily
Dreaming dreams as yet unreal?
While my parents, kith and kin
All determine my first name
I myself I must begin
To discover who I am.

I call a toast to each new baby
That somehow you will be able
To resist manipulation
To fit neatly to your station
Be yourself and stand alone
Why on earth have you been born?
Except perhaps to stand alone?

Present Time

Today and everyday
I celebrate my *birth* day
That's my present
A chance to think good thoughts
Have a shower
Dress *chic*
Make a list
Save time
So I can feel, see, smell, taste, touch
And hear everyone around me
Like a sixth sense.

Tom

I didn't know your Tom
Well, that's not true
We shook hands once and laughed on a high note
Sharing a joke about the Antarctic explorer Lawrence Oates
Before and since we passed each other by
A thousand times or more
He on his travels to work
I frequenting the Castle Park
To a world of swings and roundabouts
Where knowing it's your turn next
Makes a lot of sense.

Train Of Thought

I rush to catch that train of thought
And promptly write it down
Adrenalin determining my potpourri
Of rhyme

I'm getting quite addicted
To these hours I call my own
No disturbing signs are necessary
As I roll out of town

I think about the moments that
Embrace my sense of fun
Window-shopping in the evening
Eating out beneath the sun.

I settle on an evening
In a place without a name
A roadside full of caravans
And in their midst a game

The children are enchanted, looking in and out my car
My son is whole enraptured, watching children start a fire
A little man of ten years old but going for a song
Tips his hat at me while servilely addressing me as ma'am.

And serious he ponders ways
Of getting to the mart
And nurses us with chatter
As we wait on in the dark.

My mind rolls on to thoughts of Nell's
Minority exclusion
What motivates the hearts of men
Who revel in seclusion?

And wars go on and hurt is born
And some say "So what's new?"
And still some children disappear
With little trace or clue.

I met a friend who knows this pain
And privately we cried
Aware that none might hear us
If we dared to shout aloud.

But through our tears
We laughed and cheered each other with our warmth
And ended up discussing trends
Of coiffure colorants

And as the train is pulling in
I hum my favourite tune
And chant out fifty ways to say
"Just leave us to our fun!"

Warm Exchange

There I was
Head deep in a work report
When the phone rang.
Philip, where are you?
Outside your door
Come in, come in
Let's take a break
From busy lives
Enjoy a warm exchange
Your offering
A compilation of the best
The best of Salsa
Mine? Tea and toast
As we perused the album
And you gave me free reign
To take whatever photos I wanted
From your wonderful collection
"They can be easily replaced."

III
PERILS AND GEMS

Oh Brother!

Oh Brother, don't you know that's what you are to me
Someone to look up to, someone fine
Someone who will join with me in fun
To laugh or even scathe me with your tongue.
But then we know it's just in fun.
Oh Brother, can't you see I need your company
To lean on just while I am growing strong?
By phone we share a prayer, a secret oh so carefully
Brother I look up to you but you do not look down
You hang around
Oh Brother, hang around.

Down The Line

Strange things happen on the telephone
Revelations rocking in my ear
Silhouettes of softly silken sheen
Rushing in a non-stop mental stream.

Oh yes it must feel good to dream
The pleasures of a black-legged seam
Suspended in a mystery of lace
A fantasy just floating there in space.

Did I capture something magical in mind
When I hinted that your weakness could combine
With the feature that I know to be my strength?
Your suggestion that my limbs were something else.

Yes a few words spoken one to one
Like "This kind of thing just really turns me on"
Send us somersaulting up and down the line
When we've spoken "between lovers" on the phone.

Hail Mary

Hail Mary, say a prayer that he will phone
That my messenger will ring and ring again
And coolly I'll say "Sailor Welcome home
Come touch me with a warm familiar poem."

You're not my type, I said so from the start
But all this hype of casting out a net
In search of one such pure and perfect mate
Deserves contempt and measures second rate.

Hail Mary, is it strange for you to find
That I'm opening up so easily yet again?
The risk of getting hurt's a platitude.
I wasn't born to sit around in solitude.

Though fragile I will not develop skin
To protect and lose sight of my inner being
I'm alive and I will strive to live again
'Cause I've grown so I've lost my fear of pain.

Deep Down

I think Jacques Cousteau
Was a fine man
Deep Down

Deep Down
I know
Der Kissanne
Is a fine man

Deep Down
How well do I know
Der Kissanne?

If we were buried
Side by side
Deep Down
I'd say you're hard work

Hard work getting close to you
Hard work getting to know you
And always trying…
But where was the harm in that?

Still Waiting Meets Still Wondering

She asks him dead sincere
How clear are you about your epitaph?
"Always waiting for something to happen,"
Is his reply
Is that how he lives
Is that how he'll die?

She wants to die wondering
At the rate he waits
She probably will.
"Ah, sweet mystery of Life!"

Glory Be

Glory be to God for dimpled men
The Kissane, Kenneally and O'Connell clans
Whose smile alone can turn a maiden's head
So she can reminisce when e'er she's old
Whatever is fickle freckled
And more especially hollow
Has this strange effect upon the female mind.
Be they swift slow sweet sour adazzle dim
We fools spend half our lives
In praise of them

Driving Ms Daisy Crazy

When I'm bored of black or white or grey,
I chase a bit of colour like nature in Springtime.
My flower in bloom can be a book, a poem,
Sun on the sea or company
To set me free from Winter's gloom.

When will I learn that this new age
Is not as innocent as nature in Springtime?
That chasing cars is all the rage
Not choosing flowers.

When will I learn never again
To give my number to a stranger?
He's in the driving seat choosing to chase, or be chaste
I'm in the back seat waiting…

Next time I'll hold on to the keys
Survey the scene
And claim what's mine
The chance to turn the engine on or not

The Message Is Clear

In an ideal world
She could be swirled
Right off her feet

In an ideal world
Forever a girl
Things could be neat

When two people meet
Agendas compete
And messages blur

It's not what is fair or who deserves more
The choices are there
To do or defer, to seek or to dare to explore

So we both know the score
To expect nothing more than friendship and fun
Expect nothing less than a tender caress
And we're on…

Grace Note

I like to unwind
Stretch my mind
Exploring sound and senses
I like to rewind
Not to stop or start
But to pause
So we can replay
Our discordant notes
Eject with grace
And forward, not as a duet,
But singly in harmony
On a softer note.

Dress Code

Notes from a symphony in black
Herald the arrival of my feline persona
As I don my crushed velvet number
Fully fitted with diamante flash
I tread the boards
Inside darting back and forth like a nervous kitten
As I act out the part of a stealthy surefooted felina
Dressed to kill.

Sex Appeal

I'm appealing to men…
Some men…
Don't play games with me
Do I play games with you?
Honesty has real charm
Maybe that's why
I'm appealing to men

IV
I WISH

I Wish

I say "Are you the quiet man from Cong?"
You say "I wish."
I say "Some day I'll write for you a poem."
You say "I wish."
You say "One day I'll be a millionaire or more…"
I say "You Wish!"
You say that you've been down that road before
And you don't wish to go there anymore…
I love that bridge between the mountain and the stream
And so do I, this is no dream
We've both been here before
I say "I Wish!"

Message In A Bottle

I'll dare to sing my mermaid's song
And dare a brave man to join in
Why bottle up our gems of rhyme?
Let's open up and let them shine like sun on salty water

If a mermaid chanced to meet you
By a fountain in the park
How would you address her person?
Would you make a chance remark?

Fantasies of a mermaid swimming
Down a stretch of crystal shore
May lead on to fun and friendship
What's to lose by risking all?

Poet? Sailor? Man of courage?
Will you dare to join with me?
Delving deep to glimpse the mysteries
Lying deep within the sea

Howth Beach

I saw you on a beach at Howth
My mind adrift, your hair afloat
In a tide of dreams
You sang to me...
And I replied...the wind the sea the rock the skies
The mournful seagulls rain-filled cries
Beat in my heart like surging waves
...I hear you.

Another voice said—best take care
If you reply she'll not be there
You are too late, your song's in vain
She'll never be in Dubh Linn again.

Perhaps this is true, perhaps a lie
All I can do is write and try
My net of words may catch no maid
But that's no reason to be afraid

My song is sung, the wind has heard
Even though there may be no word
But if you're wondering what to do
Phone me John at 387102.

J.K.

Message in a Bottle RSVP

Wasn't it sweet that we should meet
Not upon a crowded street
But on a breezy sun-filled beach?

Was this some joke the Gods rehearsed?
A chance to have our roles reversed?
Were you the one enticing me
To glimpse the mysteries of the sea?

Tell me – were the mermaids singing each to each?
And did you dare to each a peach?
And wear your trousers rolled?
And did you really feel no cold?

In life do we repeat our stories
To be told and retold?
Like waves determined by the moon lapping in a
Reverending, always changing tune.

V
WORD PLAY

Word Play

He says "What will we do?"
I say "Flirt our asses off."
In a non literal literal sort of way
Like word play…before and after play
Hans 'n Mathias play.

We could pretend to dive the red wreck
In the red sea
'Til we discover that feeling déjà vu
And signal simultaneously…"We've been here before
And now we're back for more…"

More…Always wanting more
More touch more time more time to touch
More talk…More time to flirt our asses off
'Til some day one of us decides
Enough's enough…or not enough!

Nights Like This

A sedate arrangement, three to one
With enough room to squeeze in
So I did.

Balancing a silent see-saw
I juggled with my succulent beef roll
As the court jester regained control of the conversation.

Phil made her move…with grace
She sought out her advantage
As so began the musical chairs.

More see-sawing as I crossed over
And squeezed in again
To improve my view of Nancy Hunter

Momentously the men picked up the scent
As jazzy notes incited us to dance
And we went wild

No need to say a word
Desire enveloped us like fingers in a lace glove
Close but barely touching

Wild and free?
Twisting in and out of each other's grasp...
No—this was living dangerously

Smouldering kisses
Leaving a moist and lingering sensation
Longing and lingering for days...
And nights like this.

RSVP

If he's Jerry Maguire
I'm Nicole   Just kidding
Maybe that's why drop dead gorgeous
Left his bevy of beauties
To walk twenty yards in my direction
To stay long enough to be polite
By his girlfriend's watch
Yet time enough for souls to touch
So he could kiss me tenderly
Knowing I'd respond with pleasure

Close Contact

Tadgh, still fresh in mind and body
Mine and yours—yours with mine
Contact simply conceived
Through a smile a yawn
In an overheated foyer
Where John Creedon who fills my head
With warm thoughts for the day
Breathes the same hot air
Talk of fever and tracing blood
We make a link between Logan and Collins
Between stars and sea
Between you and me
'Til you're holding me so closely
Now…and then.

Fine Line

Sentences are passed between them
As they slowly check out the other
She returns to inches of dust
As the male intrusion of her territory begins in earnest.

At her request he looks at her washing line in disarray
And demands to know…"What went wrong?"
For a moment the intimacy seduces her and she shyly jokes
About her life's preoccupation with the ins and outs of washing

Designs, washing lines, are all they need to play on words
Perfect — Spice — Girl
He beckons her to look and see where she can hang her clothes
Should the occasion of sin arise.

VII

SIMPLY THE BEST

Desperate

My family are so adventurous
They couldn't see their way
To ask a stranger to carry a piece of paper
What would it weigh, one ounce?
From Kilkenny to Dublin
Without a serious introduction

And here am I, en route by train
Desperately wanting to hear Buena Vista again
To hear Buena Vista and die
Die of embarrassment at my adventurous family
Who need some introduction!

Éimear

They say you are a child of grace
And when I see that smile upon your face
I do believe that you are blessed with qualities
That happily will make this world a better place to live in.

Thank God it was inside of me that you first found
The space to grow
Until in time you deftly showed your toe
And stepped with confidence into our family tree
At once creating a new felt empathy and reverence

You have no fear of making friends
Your warm and trusting nature pays you dividends
We don't expect a loner you will be
Except perhaps occasionally

You are a child whose sensitivity will often cause you pain
Resiliently you'll have the courage
 To begin again
Along the path of your creation

And with your body you can silently express
That tenderness that first I felt
When as a baby at the breast
You fed so restfully

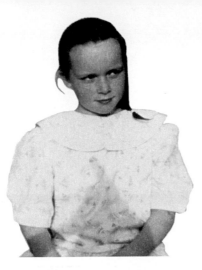

And now with some maturity
You learn sometimes impatiently
That things don't necessarily fit neatly into place
You wonder why this human race to place of work and school?

But in the evenings things slow down
And guarantee those precious times
When "Fight to-night Dad?"
Loud and clear becomes the all-familiar cheer
And Daly's Hill becomes the den
For witches, ghosts and leprechauns.

You are a child who will enthuse
When asked to make that strawberry mousse or tie a ribbon
In your hair or swim or skate without a fear of the unknown
Happily you endear yourself to every one.

Cormac

You came along with falling snow
That settled on the ground
Cormac Ruairi did we know
The treasure we had found?

You didn't care for small talk
Or making conversation
The day you asked for red sauce
Now that caused some sensation

A proud young Lego builder
Gaining confidence and fame
Getting letters from the postman
Addressed to your own name

Your first real friend was Katie
You played happily together with a love you did not hide
You just quietly reserved a place
The day that you were five

But it happened in the year ahead
As sure as melting snow
The age of innocence was dead
And time for letting go

Your life was filled with bunnies
And a certain live young hare
You guarded them so safely
Like a secret not to share

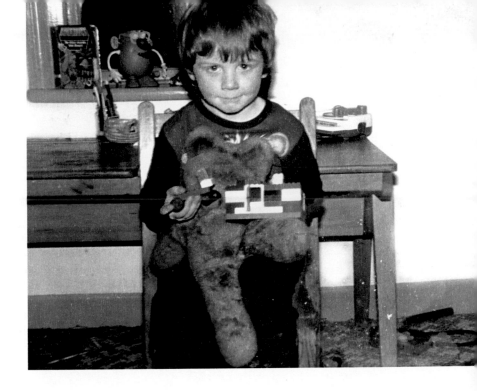

A boy among three sisters
No thorn among the rose
Whatever the occasion
You were always game to pose

You can dance and dart around us
Like a lad without a care
You like to seek attention
And remind us you are there

Yes we know we have a treasure
That arrived with falling snow
Let's hope we'll have the courage
When it's time for letting go.

Maeve

Do you believe in telepathy?
In embryo conversation
Are you aware that bonds were made
While we were in gestation?

I wonder did you somehow sense
The tension of that crochet hook
Tapping in and out of loops
In tiny heartbeat fashion.

I don't believe Noelle could guess
That we would nightly think of her
As little fingers happily caress each square
That she so patiently addressed with care.

And how did you enjoy
Jumping in and out of pools?
And settling in the warm jacuzzi
And then dear Maeve you braved the elements of February.

Together we anticipated an all-embracing welcome
Feeling warm and certain we are safely home.
A moving moment captured in a blaze of colour
So refreshing after hours of pure and perfect Persiled power.

And now we watch you
Crawling in and out of danger zones
When you are twenty-one will you look coyly up at me?
And seek out my approval?

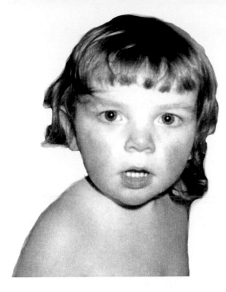

You waken up in early morning cheer
And wave your limbs all four in my direction
And with your fingers you explore
You plat du jour with satisfaction.

And then you join in family fun
Like now when Éimear sings aloud the bridal tune
"Here she comes" her dress held high
Revealing bottom bare and thigh

Our little dark-haired one!
We welcome you to join with us
And sing our tune
In frenzied unison.

Gráinne

Gráinne love, you're three tomorrow
How do you feel about that?
Is this the end of the terrible twos,
Or will we have to have a chat?

You emerged in all your glory
On a Tuesday morning early
And since then the utter magic
Leaves us sometimes captivated
And the taunting and the torment
Leaves us sometimes sheer frustrated

You're a powerful little woman
We're all dancing to your tune
Twinkle twinkle little star
Sure we love you as you are
And we wonder will you wander
Will you wonder who you are?
If your christening were tomorrow
Would we call you Auntie Marie?
Or would Bossy Boots be closer
To the bone?

Tonight Leonie spoke of you
A little girl who's still just two
With confidence and courage
That is surely all your own.

Beloved Son

I could say
There's my beloved son in whom
I'm well pleased
Or I could say you'd never mistake
The big head of him
Even through two thick Iarnrod Eireann windows
Across which no sound will pass
I did try
But if it wasn't for Gráinne
I could not have looked him in the eye
Or helped create that hilarious
Exchange of laughter
That always but too seldom
Occurs at holiday time
When we're all at our best
Happy with the world
And loving one another
As a beloved son
And his beloved mother

Words of Wisdom

What's a crossword nana?
Oisín that's the question
You posed today
If only you never
Had to know what a cross word is

Crossed words
Crossed wires
Crossing over

You believe in magic
But now and again
Reality begins to dawn
Like last night when
Teddy was tucked in beside you
And you remarked "I wish teddy had feelings"
You discover new things
Every minute of every day

Like lately you
Announced to all
Guess what! I was born
On my birthday WOW!
And as you sit on the loo in your birthday suit
And I tell you
One day you'll laugh about that
You as good as promise
That this is no laughing matter
And never will be.

It's okay you say
To sit on the loo in
Your birthday suit
Doing what comes naturally
Over and over *you* show *us*
The way to go.

VII
CUT 2 CHASE

Cut 2 Chase

Slow manoeuvres
Fast rotation
Swap a lady
On the double
Recognition
Bits exchanged
Stops before me
Hand on button
Hesitates
Nothing said
No exchange
Sound barrier

Lines between deliberating

Couldn't make it
Better offer
Eyes meet
Firm exchange
Frontal touch
See you Monday
Thrilling moment
Replayed
Backtracking
Same old story
Re-written
No denial
Favourite speak
Blow your hair back

Word compelling
Verbal fencing
Razor sharp
Moments stolen
Love 1
2 All
Replay
S'il vous plait

Reality check months later

Touching moment
Intuition
Learning process
Need to know
Cut to chase
Cover blown
Risking face
Yet again
Risking fire
Please do
Translate
As I say
Mind Blowing
As you like it
My pleasure
On the day.

Overnight Celeb!

Cool reggae music in the heat of the day
Beats out the rhythm to the ocean way
Turquoise and yellow create a swell scene
As a charming cool Jamaican is caressing my skin

The ambiance is shattered by a cold piercing ring
It's 9.30 in the morning and I haven't done a thing
Is that Brenda who is chatting on the radio show?
She's asking all us singles where's the place to go.

The place to mingle, the place to ensnare
The place to make music and places to beware
I listen as I gaze out at the Summer morning mist
And since nothing new is happening I decide to enlist

The numbers are a jumble but I manage to get through
The researcher's enervated when I tell her what I do
She says expect a call from a bod at the top
My adrenalin starts rising 'til it's racing now non-stop

I have minutes left to think my initiative through
Is this the sort of thing that I really want to do?
Declare to the nation what my love life is not
That without intervention I'm a sad old swot?

'Cause I've studied this scene for a decade or so
Been courted by desirables desiring something new
But whatever we are looking for it's hard to realise
Unless of course it's lurking there confused and in disguise

And as I try to fathom what it is I need to say
To the nation and whoever else is listening on the day
My routine takes a hike while my energy is spent
In an effort to sound sexy and superbly eloquent.

Imagine that my children could be listening to the show
Never mind extended family, clientele, my friends and foe
But in juggling will I, won't I, I prioritise my goal
What good is reggae music if you ain't got soul

But dreams of becoming a new overnight celeb
Have been shattered by a telephone that's suddenly gone dead
I haven't booked a flight yet to Jamaica in the sun
For caresses from my lover with the reggae music on

But a turning point directs me now to take it nice and slow
Make male friends of the calibre of female friends I know
To you men who want an intro to us women warm with charm
Extend the hand of friendship and let's go there arm in arm.

Voodoophone Taboo

I said I'd postpone
The conceivable evil
 Of mobilised phone

Tho' nobody said
It incites sibling strife
Or lowers de tone

Nobody spoke
Of textosterone toll
Taking over my life

Nobody warned
It's like falling in lust
Overnight

Nobody said
I could have so much fun
In bed on my own

Nobody said
That the unwritten word
Could be riddled with dangerous zones

Nobody said
I'd feel pain in my heart
Like a dart from an arrow and bow

Nobody said
Let your heart rule your head
In a transient moment of bliss

Nobody said
You could coast all night long
Without even a kiss

Nobody said
You'd be wrecking my head
With your rockin' and rollin' on words

Nobody told me
I could be bold
Over and over again

Nobody said
That Confucious rules
'Til you don't know your R's from your Zeros

Nobody said
That my pulse rate might quicken
'Til I might explode

Could you or I guess
At your lit'ral conquest
Landing *idir* these covers and sheets?

Nobody could guess
This erotic excess
As one word thrives on another

Exorcise 'n destress
Regain power more or less
I dabble in words of composure

Words to hum and to hue
To construct and construe
Quote Katie Melu…
Ah…dis aphrodisiac…'tis U!

Recordo d'Italia

Dearest Dervla, I was there
Having packed my runners and my underwear
Fired with vigour on this virgin flight
My lips touched down on the landing site.

Derv I'm not sure if I'm in the mood
To write down lines to be misconstrued
But hell I think I'll have a go
To capture the crew of this holy damned show.

Well Sue she sang like a bird on a tree
We sure felt proud at the embassy
And Frances from Howth showed incredible flair
As she did her stint as a courier.

Now Des I think he's a real teddy bear
He's kind and considerate and far too fair
For as he made sure we were all on our way
His own damned taxi went the opposite way.

And Tom was the one who really stole the show
When it comes to entertainment and just letting go
Leg walking muscles not a moment's pain
But belly aching laughter caused a hell of a strain

Eithne she has been roomin' with me
She says I snore like a bumble bee
She came in one night, and found me in the bed
So early that she thought that I must be dead

Congrats Dingle Dangler for that wordy game
John A. means more than just J.A.M?
But what about Ali and his forty thieves
Why didn't you commend an cigire?

I could go on and fill up the page
About Denis the Menace and his entourage
Now Eamonn I think wouldn't say a bad word
But his hands said it all and maybe that's good

'Cause it just might happen
That Inspector Morse
Might move him from the drug scene
To something worse.

Like moving the traffic with his bare little hands
While saying that it's legal when you're in demand
On a busy day in the neighbourhood
And you know that you do it for the common good.

Rosalie's the girl who sells lingerie
She doesn't give a damn about privacy
She came in one day invaded my room
Re-arranged my elastic 'til it went boom boom

So back to the start of that crazy crew
There was Jo and her son – well we all went phew!
But just as it happened our luck wasn't in
'Cos the cool looking dude was just leaving Mam in.

Now as I sat on that aeroplane
I was feeling kind of funny betwixt and between
A singer and a soldier with a bad old leg
But he kept pulling mine 'til I said "Hey Jude."

We walked on the hills and we paved the way
For the next pilgrimage on the Appian Way
We panted and sweated but we all turned in
For the buzzin' and the boozin' and the drinkin' of gin

Well it's Ciao from me and Ciao from you
The needle's getting stuck and I don't know what to do
I'll have to take a jump just to let you all know
Like your one in Tosca from Castleangelo...
That was her way of saying
It's the end of the show

Maureen McDonnell has recently finished studying photography in Dublin and at Bradford College.
More of her sea collection is available on the portfolio section of the website of the Royal Photographic Society.

Ann Moloney graduated with First Class Honours from the Limerick College of Art. She has exhibited at the RHA and other national and international venues and has been continuously involved in the art world, painting and selling, selling and painting.

Email: mols@yahoo.com
Tel: 061 302 929

ABOUT THE AUTHOR

Anne Murphy was born in Co. Down. She has four children and one grandson. She lives and works in Kilkenny. She is a graduate of Queen's University Belfast and The University of Aberdeen. She recently completed a Certificate in Print Journalism, a Kilkenny VEC and *Kilkenny People* initiative. She is currently working on her collection of short stories.

Email Anne at:
annesmurff@gmail.com

Access Anne's blog:
annesmurff@livejournal.com